## KEVIN DYER

Kevin is an experienced playwright with over 40 commissioned plays behind him. He has recently written a new *Beauty and the Beast* for The Dukes Play-in-the-Park, *The Monster Under The Bed* for Polka, and *The Fool on the Hill* for Action Transport Theatre.

Kevin is the Associate Writer for Action Transport Theatre; a professional writer embedded in a new-writing company. He leads creative writing sessions, works as a dramaturg for other writers and leads collective-writing processes where a dozen or more writers share their creativity to make surprising new plays.

He also works as a director and an actor. He is a published poet, has reviewed cinema and books, judged literary competitions and has worked as a journalist on papers and magazines.

When Kevin was 10, Peter Fox - his primary school teacher - typed up a story he had written. The story won no prizes and never will, but Peter Fox gave him the encouragement to be a writer. (He also taught him how to catch one-handed, make battleships out of balsa wood and kick a ball with his left foot.)

You can contact Kevin Dyer at:
writing@actiontransporttheatre.co.uk or
kevindyer@tiscali.co.uk

**Action Transport Theatre Company
and The Dukes Lancaster**

present

# THE BOMB

by

## Kevin Dyer

AURORA METRO PRESS

First printed in 2005 by Aurora Metro Publications Ltd.
Reprinted in 2006 and 2008.
www.aurorametro.com  Tel: 020 3 261 0000 info@aurorametro.com
*The Bomb* © copyright Kevin Dyer 2008
Interview with Jo Berry and Pat Magee © copyright The Forgiveness Project.
New writing information and interviews © copyright Action Transport Theatre
Co. 2005.

Trade distribution:
UK - Central Books Tel: 020 8986 4854 orders@centralbooks.com
USA - Theatre Communications Group, N.Y. Tel: 212 609 5900 tcg@tcg.org
Canada - Playwrights Union of Canada Tel: 416 703 0013
orders@playwrightscanada.com
Printed by Ashford Colour Press, Fareham, Hants, UK.
ISBN 09546912-7-X  978-09546912-7-1

*With thanks to*
*Jo Berry and Pat Magee,*
*working for peace,*
*working for change.*

**Action Transport**

22 years of making brilliant new theatre locally, nationally and internationally, *for*, *by* and *with* young people.

Action Transport Theatre commissioned *The Bomb* for production in spring 2006 for schools touring and autumn 2006 for a UK theatres tour.

The 2006 tour of *The Bomb* was one of my last projects as Action Transport Theatre's General Manager. I am delighted to be returning to both the company, in my new role as Director, and *The Bomb*, in its third touring production.

Action Transport Theatre believes that good theatre develops the imagination, encourages empathy and connects people to the world in which they live. *The Bomb* does all of these things and more. It has been a privilege for the company to work with two extraordinary people, Jo Berry and Pat Magee, and to enable audiences of young people and adults to experience such a powerful story through the world of our play.

We are very pleased to be co-producing this tour with The Dukes, Lancaster and we warmly welcome you, our audience, as you join us for *The Bomb*.

**Sarah Clover, Director**

Touring 2008:

**31st October – 1st November**
The Baby Grand
Grand Opera House, Belfast
Box Office 028 9024 1919
**6th November**
University of Hertfordshire,
Hatfield
Box Office 01707 281127
**10th-11th November**
Warwick Arts Centre, Coventry
Box Office 024 7652 4524
**12th-13th November**
Theatre by the Lake, Keswick
Box Office 017687 74411

Coming Next:
*The Mask* - an extraordinary play about two ordinary kids
written collectively by North West writers. Touring February –
March 2009.

*Generations* – an intergenerational, theatre production for
summer 2009 in Ellesmere Port.

*Fool on the Hill* – a new play with puppets by Kevin Dyer which
looks at old age and childhood and turns dementia and old age
on their head. Touring nationally autumn 2009.

www.actiontransporttheatre.co.uk

the
**Dukes**
Lancaster

The Dukes is a unique cultural centre for Lancashire existing to create and produce great theatre and act as a centre for film and digital arts, dance, music and the performing arts.

*The Bomb* will be our first production to play in The Round, our new studio theatre, before touring across the UK. It's an example of our desire to make modern plays about the world we live in, plays which appeal across the generations. Whether you're 15 or 50, we hope you'll be moved and inspired by the production.

Working on the play with Jo and Pat has had a profound effect on the creative team. There's both a sense of challenge and obligation here - we know we are making a fiction, a work of the imagination, but we also know that real events and real lives have inspired the play. The job for us is to try to do justice to the source material by creating a great theatrical experience.

There's a challenge for the audience too. *The Bomb* is hard-hitting and asks some difficult questions; as the credit crunch hits, shouldn't we really be doing comedies and musicals, guaranteeing 'a good night out?' Well, we will do comedies and probably musicals too, but for now we are going to a deeper place. If you accept the idea that a great play can shift your view, change your perception, then *The Bomb* may challenge you in just the right way.

**Joe Sumsion, Director**

## Coming Soon

### *What's Cooking?*

### Thursday 29 January – Saturday 21 February 2009
### *Sabbat* by Richard Shannon

A new play telling the gripping story of Alice Nutter, one of the Lancashire Witches tried and executed in Lancaster 400 years ago.

### Thursday 19 March – Saturday 11 April 2009
### *Jamaica House* by Paul Sirett

A funny and moving drama set on the twelfth floor of an empty tower block.

www.dukes-lancaster.org

Promoting City, Coast & Countryside

<u>Autumn 2008</u>
<u>Cast List</u>

| | |
|---|---|
| Elizabeth | Janys Chambers |
| Marnie /Lizzie/The woman on the ferry | Abigail Hood |
| Ned Keenan | Paul Dodds |
| William Townshend MP | John Mawson |

<u>Production Team</u>

| | |
|---|---|
| Director | Joe Sumsion |
| Designer | Alison Heffernan |
| Composer | Julian Ronnie |
| Stage Manager on Tour | Mike Francis |
| Lighting Designer | Mike Francis |
| Deputy Stage Manager | Vicky Laker |

<u>For Action Transport Theatre:</u>

| | |
|---|---|
| Director | Sarah Clover |
| Associate Writer | Kevin Dyer |
| Company Producer | Jessica Egan |
| Production Manager | Mike Francis |
| Associate Director | Nina Hajiyianni |
| General Manager | Karen Parry |

<u>For the Dukes, Lancaster:</u>

| | |
|---|---|
| Director | Joe Sumsion |
| Finance Manager | Pat Russell |
| Finance Assistant | Elaine Cooper |
| Theatre Secretary | Jacqui Wilson |
| Film Programme Manager | Leon Gurevitch |
| Production & Operations Manager | John Newman-Holden |
| Stage Manager | Graeme Brown |

| | |
|---|---|
| Deputy Stage Manager | Vicky Laker |
| Assistant Stage Manager | Sophia Horrocks |
| Chief Technician | Brent Lees |
| Deputy Technician | John Bates |
| Assistant Technicians | Amy Clarey |
| Projectionist | Jonathon Ilot |
| Wardrobe Supervisor | Ann Preston |
| Wardrobe Deputy | Susan Wright |
| Marketing Manager | Jonathan Gilchrist |
| Marketing/Press Officer | Maria Major |
| Producer | Julie Brown |
| Creative Learning Director | Guy Christiansen |
| Assist. Creative Learning Dir. | Wren Chapman |
| Youth Theatre Leaders | Leonard St Jean, Emma Friend |
| Box Office Manager | Karen Chandisingh |
| Box Office Assistants | Peter Button, Sam Kaey, Leon Gurevitch, Mary Sharples |
| Front of House Manager | Andrew Carruthers |
| Duty Managers | Peter Button, Christopher World, Dawn Chadwick, Andrew Kayll |
| Bar staff & attendants | Ruby Clarke, Tom Diffenthal, LLorer Foulger, Anna Friewald, Sharon Hall, Bridget Halldearn, Mary Sharples, Gary Smith, Mia Wilson, Ruth Davidson, Tim Forster, Jacqui Wilson, Tim Sanderson, Jemma Smith, Joe Shepherd, Aileen Menzies. |
| Lancashire CC Young People's Service | Richard Whyman, Guy Morris, Kate Greenway |
| Honorary Archivist | Bernard Gladstone |
| Production Photographer | George Coupe |
| Audio Describer | Anne Hornsby |
| BSL Interpreter | Kyra Pollitt |
| Theatre Chaplain | Rev Hayley Matthews |

# BIOGRAPHIES

## The Cast

**JANYS CHAMBERS - Elizabeth**
Theatre includes: *Wuthering Heights*/*Amadeus*/the musical *It's a Girl* (Chester Gateway); Macbeth (Theatre Foundry); Cinderella (Library Theatre); On *The Plastic* (Birmingham Rep); *It's A Girl* (again!) /*The Pope And The Witch* (West Yorkshire Playhouse); *Stevie*/*Educating Rita* (Theatr Colwyn); *Equus* (Northampton Royal); *Lear's Daughters* (2 national tours); *East Is East* (Bolton/York national tour); *These Things Do Happen* (York Royal); *Tinder Box* (KneeHigh); *Snow Queen* (Action Transport) and *Tom Sawyer* (Dukes' Lancaster).
TV includes: *Coronation Street*/*Brookside*/*Hetty Wainthropp*/*The Royal Today*/*Courtroom*/*Always and Everyone*/*Dalziel and Pascoe*/*Out of Hours*/*Butterfly Collector*.
Radio includes *Frankenstein,* and *Sons and Lovers.*
Janys has written over fifty plays for theatre and radio; published four; written for *Holby*/*Children's Ward*/ *Engie Bengy;* and *Emmerdale* for 5 years. Her episode represented the BBC series *Belonging* when it won a BAFTA. She's received nominations for Best New Writer for Television, Best Episode in a Soap, and Best Radio Play for Children. She was runner-up in the Greenwich International Poetry Competition.
As Associate Artist at The New Vic, she directed *A Christmas Carol*, and *Pat and Margaret*, also directing for Oldham Coliseum/Theatre Centre/ Perspectives/countless youth theatres. She loves young people's work, and teaching.

**PAUL DODDS** – Ned Keenan

Since graduating from The Oxford School of Drama, Paul has worked for many theatre companies including M6, New Perspectives, Travelling Light and Walking Forward and is immensely proud of his ongoing association with Action Transport. His Television Credits include: *The Bill*, Catherine Cookson's *A Dinner of Herbs* and *Peak Practice*. He is delighted to be re-touring with *The Bomb*. He was nominated as Best Actor for his role in *The Bomb* at the TMA Awards 2006.

**ABIGAIL HOOD** – Marnie/ Lizzie/ the woman on the ferry

After achieving a degree in Drama and Theatre Studies from Middlesex University Abigail went on to train at the Oxford School of Drama. Since graduating, her theatre work has included extensive touring with the Ape Theatre Company, *Mary Queen of Scots Got Her Head Chopped Off* (Pegasus Theatre), *Epsom Downs* (Cockpit Theatre), *Godspell* (Edinburgh Fringe Festival 2006), *Faultlines* (Union Theatre), *Deathline* (Old Red Lion), *Charley's Aunt* (Wimbledon Studio Theatre), *Weapons of Happiness* at the Finborough Theatre and, most recently, a number of site-specific performances with physical theatre company Tangled Feet. Also, Abigail was last year part of the original cast of *That Face* at the Royal Court.

**JOHN MAWSON – William Townshend MP**
Recent theatre credits: Max Wax in the musical *Loving Art* at the Landor Theatre, Benjamin Braun in *The Gaelic Teacher* at the Etcetera Theatre, Mr Moore in *Pages* for the New Writing Collective at the Pacific Playhouse, Dr Dorn in *The Seagull* and various roles in *What's Left Behind/Mamenshka* for Act Provocateur at the Lion and Unicorn, Friedrich Hofreiter in Stoppard's *Undiscovered Country* at the New Players Theatre, Dr Astrov in *Uncle Vanya* directed by Hugh Fraser, Corporal Nym and Williams in *Henry V* directed by Joe Harmston for Tour De Force. He trained at The Actors Company at LCTS. Before turning professional, John enjoyed careers as a Master Mariner in the Merchant Navy and then in shipping insurance.

## Production Team

**JOE SUMSION – Director**
Following a Drama Degree at Bristol University Joe worked as a freelance director for companies including M6 Theatre Company, The Dukes, Nottingham Playhouse, Manchester Youth Theatre, the Royal Theatre, Northampton and Theatre Royal Stratford East. Between 2001 and 2007 Joe was Artistic Director of Action Transport, commissioning and directing many plays including three co-productions with Vulavulani Theatre Company, South Africa. In 2007, Joe edited *The Skeleton Key*, a book sharing the secrets of creating outstanding plays made *for* and *by* young people. Joe has just directed *Beauty and the Beast* in Williamson Park, his first show as Director of the Dukes. TMA Awards Nominee - Best Director for *The Bomb* (2006), Winner - Writers' Guild New Writing Encouragement Award for *The Bomb* (2006).

**ALISON HEFFERNAN** – Designer

Assoc. Artist of Action Transport whose previous designs include: *Night Train*, *Fly Away Peter*, *The Bomb* (previous tours) and *Scorcher*. Other recent theatre includes: *Beauty and the Beast* for The Dukes Lancaster and *Dick Barton*, *Union Street*, *Albert Nobbs*, *Women on the Verge of HRT*, *Wind in the Willows* (Winner M.E.N. Award for Best Family Production 2005 and nominated for Best Design) *A Little Local Difficulty* and *Mail Order Bride*, all for Oldham Coliseum. Productions include *Hue Boy*, and *My Place* for Tutti Frutti and *Silly Billy*, and *Jack* for Tutti Frutti/York Theatre Royal, *Jaz and Flo* (a large scale sensory installation for 3-5 year olds), *Danny King of the Basement*, *On the Street Where I live* and *Odd Socks* for M6 Theatre Company. Other work includes costume design for *Dance Passion* and *Apassionata* on board the QM2, QE2 and Queen Victoria Cunard ships; Assoc. Designer at the Royal Theatre Northampton, small-scale tours and TIE for New Perspectives, Royal Theatre Touring and Sheffield Theatres; Production Designer for Brookside. She originally trained in sculpture and then at the Motley Design Course at Riverside Studios under Margaret Harris.

**MIKE FRANCIS** – Lighting Designer / Stage Manager on Tour

Mike Francis joined Action Transport for the tour of *Mrs Noah and The Flood* in 2002 and went on to spend four weeks touring *Dumisani's Drum* to schools in Soweto in the Summer of 2003 and hasn't looked back since!

**JULIAN RONNIE – Composer**
Recently Julian has written the music for the
BAFTA award winning Channel 4 Series
*Skins*, as well as *Vice, Peak Practice,
Everyman, House Doctor, Scene Stealers,
Six Nations Rugby, Inside Sport, The Pride of
Britain Awards* and the new *Channel 5 News*
theme tune with Natasha Kaplinsky. He
provided the score for *Parallels* a new movie
which has just premiered at Cannes and has written literally
hundreds of TV commercials including Famous Grouse,
Sainsbury's, Crusha (just released as a single) and Pepsi. For
the theatre, Julian wrote the music for the critically acclaimed
productions of *Tom Sawyer* and *Ay Carmela,* performed at the
Contact Theatre in Manchester; as well as for *Dr Jekyll & Mr
Hyde, Broken Angel* and *Flat Stanley* for the West Yorkshire
Playhouse. For Action Transport he wrote the music for *Mrs
Noah and the Flood, Warrior Square* and *Who's Breaking.* His
musical adaptation of the Canterville Ghost, *Curses! – The
Farcical* directed by Bob Carlton in Hornchurch was awarded
"Best Musical off West End." His new musical *GRIM - Hard
Core Fairy Tales* is due to open in the West End in 2009.
www.mammothmusic.co.uk

## New Writing at Action Transport

Since 2001, Action Transport has been exploring the gap between making new plays *for* young people and making new plays *by* young people. In 2003, Kevin Dyer was appointed as Associate Writer with a particular brief to encourage young writers and keep new writing at the heart of the company. Here, he talks about the company's work:

'For twenty years Action Transport has been producing touring productions for children and young people. New writing has been central to the best work of the Company. It now *only* produces new work and at its heart are creative relationships with professional writers.

We commission professional writers to write plays. We also work with many fired-up young writers who have something to say. What is happening more and more in the company is the connection of these two strands. We are no longer simply delivering drama to young people, we have a wider, deeper writing belief.

*Raver 2005*
*Written and devised by Youth Theatre members and young writers*
*Photo: Sylvia Selzer*

We now make plays *for, by* and *with* young people –
sometimes all at once – and this mix of professional and
emerging writers is key to the company's success. We
connect the two in order to embed the experience of
young people in our commissioned touring work. We also
know that working with young writers benefits the
professional writers who do it. At the same time, we are
creating a new generation of writers. Our young writers
are on a sort of informal apprenticeship; they work
alongside writers already familiar with the business of
creating, developing and pitching ideas.

*Spike 2005*
*Written by a group of young writers with Kevin Dyer*
*Photo: Sylvia Selzer*

An example of this mixing of professional and
developing writers is my own experience on *The Bomb*.
The first people to read it weren't the folk who were going
to produce it, but a small group from *Action Transport
Writers* who were just beginning to write their own plays,
were doing GCSEs and A levels and who were the same
age and voice as the young woman in my play. Invaluable.

During my writing and re-writing of the play I have called on young writers to read it many times – so they can observe my process for *their* learning – and so that they can tell *me* how to make my play better.

Increasingly, more experienced and new writers will work on the same project. *Action Transport Writers*, for example, is a selected group of writers with a range of abilities and experience. It includes writers who have had work produced on Radio 4, creative-writing graduates, and younger writers still at school. We work together on how to write better – and the company supports them on their own individual projects. One of them, John Moorhouse, has written a play that is so impressive it was bought by the company and received a full professional tour in 2007.

*Kidnapped 2005*
*Youth Theatre Production*
*Photo: Sylvia Selzer*

It takes a million decisions to get a play from first idea to stage. That is why plays often fizzle out, miss the target, and don't quite cut the mustard. But sometimes enough of those decisions are the right ones and something amazing, life-changing happens.

My job is to mentor professional and young writers; imagine, develop and lead writing projects; and to keep new writing at the heart of the company. We run open access sessions, master classes and also sessions examining the writing and creation of all our made work – usually to invited writers. We are always on the look out for young people who want to try their hand at writing their own plays.'

*Birdboy by Nick Wood*
*co-produced with Nottingham Playhouse Roundabout*
*photo: Sammyco*

## Jo Berry and Patrick Magee

*Patrick Magee and Jo Berry*
*Photograph by permission of Jo Berry*

When Sir Anthony Berry MP was killed in the IRA Brighton Bombing during the 1984 Tory Party Conference, his daughter, Jo, was thrown into a conflict she knew very little about. Since then she has visited Ireland many times and worked with victims and former combatants from all sides. In November 2000, she met Pat Magee, the man responsible for her father's death.

Belfast-born Pat Magee, former IRA activist, was given multiple life sentences for the Brighton Bombing. Released under the Good Friday Agreement in 1999, he has since been actively involved in peace work. In 2003, with Jo's help, he set up Causeway, a healing project that helps individuals address unresolved pain caused by The Troubles.

**Jo Berry**: An inner shift is required to hear the story of the enemy. For me the question is always about whether I can let go of my need to blame, and open my heart enough to hear Pat's story and understand his motivations. The truth is that sometimes I can and sometimes I can't. It's a journey and it's a choice, which means it's not all sorted and put away in a box.

It felt as if a part of me died in that bomb. I was totally out of my depth but somehow I held on to a small hope that something positive would come out of the trauma. So I went to Ireland and listened to the stories of many remarkable and courageous people who'd been caught up in the violence. For the first time I felt that my pain was being heard.

In those early years I probably used the word 'forgiveness' too liberally – I didn't really understand it. When I used the word on television, I was shocked to receive a death threat from a man who said I had betrayed both my father and my country.

Now I don't talk about forgiveness. To say, "I forgive you", is almost condescending – it locks you into an 'us and them' scenario keeping me right and you wrong. That attitude won't change anything. But I can experience empathy, and in that moment there is no judgment. Sometimes when I've met with Pat, I've had such a clear understanding of his life that there's nothing to forgive.

I wanted to meet Pat to put a face to the enemy, and see him as a real human being. At our first meeting I was terrified, but I wanted to acknowledge the courage it had taken him to meet me. We talked with an extraordinary intensity. I shared a lot about my father, while Pat told me some of his story.

Over the past two and a half years of getting to know Pat, I feel I've been recovering some of the humanity I lost when that bomb went off. Pat is also on a journey to recover his humanity. I know that he sometimes finds it hard to live with the knowledge that he cares for the daughter of someone he killed through his terrorist actions.

Perhaps more than anything I've realised that no matter which side of the conflict you're on, had we all lived each other's lives, we could all have done what the other did. In other words, had I come from a Republican background, I could easily have made the same choices Pat made.

**Pat Magee**: Some day I may be able to forgive myself. Although I still stand by my actions, I will always carry the burden that I harmed other human beings. But I'm not seeking forgiveness. If Jo could just understand why someone like me could get involved in the armed struggle then something has been achieved. The point is that Jo set out with that intent in mind – she wanted to know why.

I decided to meet Jo because, apart from addressing a personal obligation, I felt obligated as a Republican to explain what led someone like me to participate in the action. I told her that I'd got involved in the armed struggle at the age of 19, after witnessing how a small nationalist community were being mistreated by the British. Those people had to respond. For 28 years I was active in the Republican Movement. Even in jail I was still a volunteer.

Between Jo and I, the big issue is the use of violence. I can't claim to have renounced violence, though I don't believe I'm a violent person and have spoken out against it. I am a hundred per cent in favour of the peace process, but I am not a pacifist and I could never say to future generations, anywhere in the world, who felt themselves oppressed, "Take it, just lie down and take it."

Jo told me that her daughter had said after one of our meetings, "Does that mean that Grandad Tony can come back now?" It stuck with me, because of course nothing has fundamentally changed. No matter what we can achieve as two human beings meeting after a terrible event, the loss remains and forgiveness can't embrace that loss. The hope lies in the fact that we are prepared to carry on. The dialogue has continued.

It's rare to meet someone as gracious and open as Jo. She's come a long way in her journey to understanding: in fact, she's come more than half way to meet me. That's a very humbling experience.

For other stories of forgiveness, and information about
The Forgiveness Project
visit:

www.theforgivenessproject.com

## Sarah Clover, Action Transport Theatre, talks with Jo Berry 2006

**Sarah:** What motivated you to share your story with Kevin Dyer as writer, and support Action Transport in producing *The Bomb*?

**Jo:** I don't have any rules at all about which projects I get involved in. Kevin approached me after attending the 20th Anniversary of the Brighton Bomb, in London. He shared what he was wanting to do by writing *The Bomb* and I immediately felt a trust with him, I had a totally good feeling, I suppose it's intuition. I just felt this was something I wanted to explore. I have turned down other projects. It usually takes me a bit of time to feel whether it is right.

Something Kevin said really struck me, he wanted to write a play that wasn't about being true to the outer events, but he wanted to have integrity with the feelings, so that people watching it would feel some of the feelings I would have felt. He really wanted to understand the emotional journey I'd been through and I felt we had a shared language, which was important. I found out more about Action Transport through meeting Joe [Sumsion, Artistic Director]. I think the Company has wonderful values, and is inspiring, and I was really excited about the opportunity of working together.

**Sarah:** Kevin wanted to focus on your emotional journey: do you feel that he's achieved that now you've seen drafts of the script?

**Jo:** I will only really know that totally when I see the play. Having read the final draft I am happy that the integrity is there. It is true to the spirit of my story. I'm very happy with how it's going.

**Sarah:** *The Bomb* is inspired by your story up until your meeting with Pat. Is there more of your journey after that meeting you would like to share with us?

**Jo:** Five years on, we are now friends and it's taken quite a long time for me to be able to say that and not feel that I am betraying my father or my family. We've shared so much together and there's a lot of caring on each side. That sometimes can be quite difficult because it feels like there's so much taboo about meeting someone who has killed your loved one and you mustn't start caring about them! It's still challenging. It's not like meeting someone normal, like meeting my mates, nothing like that, there's always an extra dimension.

We recently went to Austria together to an international conference where people weren't so directly involved with the conflict in Northern Ireland. They had less ideas about us both, and that meant we were freer to talk, rather than worrying about whether we were upsetting people, that was very interesting and helpful for our dialogue. In Northern Ireland or England there's always one group that might be upset by what we say.

**Sarah:** I wonder if *The Bomb* will create a similar feeling of freedom with the young people who see it and who will have less experience of the IRA?

**Jo**: What is interesting is that I have found that people make our story their own, they relate to it in their life. I'm sure for young people they are very aware of the risk of new terrorism and experience their own feelings about this. Also I think everyone has experienced someone in their life who is bullying them or threatening them. Everyone has been hurt, or has hurt others. The choice is how we live with that, how we deal with it. It is also important to me that I feel all my feelings even the difficult ones like anger. I have found that with anger I have a choice whether to use it to hurt others or to use it to empower myself.

**Sarah**: What difference has it made to you to be able to meet Pat?

**Jo**: It has made a big difference to meet Pat as now I see him as a real human being rather than the 'enemy'. I am grateful for the opportunity to go on a journey with him and now know that this journey is helping others, which in turn helps me. If something positive comes out of my father's death then it helps make sense of it for me. If I hadn't met Pat then I know I would have found other ways to bring something positive out of the bomb. I did not base my healing on meeting him – in fact I thought it would never happen and, if it did, it would only be one meeting. When I heard he would meet me, I didn't have much warning I only knew for sure in the morning.

**Sarah**: Which is echoed in *The Bomb*?

**Jo**: That is right, it is true, I really was just making the soup, cleaning the house. And what I was thinking on the ferry was, well, it's a one-off meeting, that's it. He was there to defend his position. Half-way through he just stopped talking, took off his glasses, and said, 'I just don't know what to say. I've never met anyone with as much dignity as you. What can I do to help?' That's when I realised it was just the start of another journey, not the end. When I left the incredibly intense meeting I said I'm so glad it's you. What I meant was he was prepared to go on a journey with me. I couldn't have predicted that.

I couldn't tell others how to do it. All I can say is it's about little steps, you'll know your next step, and others can help you find that within you. No one can say you should be feeling this or doing this. It isn't about that.

**Sarah**: Your story is very inspiring to others.

**Jo**: It's about inspiring and empowering others. As others have inspired me to do what I've needed to do. Like Peaceful Tomorrows in America, and the many groups of people I've met, some I haven't met, who have helped me to do what I've needed to do. I haven't done this on my own, a huge number of people have helped. I don't feel isolated at all.

**Sarah**: Is there anything specific you would like audiences to take away from the play besides your story, your inspiration?

**Jo**: No one needs to stay a victim, everyone can go on a journey of healing however difficult the situation. There are always alternatives to blaming which can heal the pain without continuing the cycle of violence and revenge.

**Sarah**: How will you be linking *The Bomb* to your own peace work?

**Jo**: It is totally aligned with my peace work and my passion. It will become a major focus for my work next year. I don't know how far it is going to go but it's very important. It will be a strand along with working with Peaceful Tomorrows, and the Parents Circle in Israel, where bereaved families from both sides are doing incredible work, helping dialogue between the Palestinians and the Israelis and doing a lot of work with young people as well. I am going to London in a few days to help launch a ministry of peace; I go back to Ireland a lot, doing things there. I am also writing my book with Pat. Every month is different. That's the wonderfulness of this work, the possibilities that can happen.

**Sarah**: Does it make a particular difference *The Bomb* being focused for young people?

**Jo**: Very much so. It is a new area for me to tell my story. I am very excited that it's coming through the medium of this play and being made accessible to young people. I feel very lucky that I have the opportunity to listen to young people and find out what they are feeling about the world, and war and politics and peace. It feels like young people rarely get a chance just to share their story, their experience, and be heard without anyone evaluating or judging or fitting it into the curriculum. But actually just sharing. All young people have a story, which is valid and powerful and important. Others need to hear them. They deserve to have their story heard, not just adults.

It would be wonderful if schools saw the need for young people to share their stories. You need a lot of emotional safety and confidentiality. My workshops linking to *The Bomb* will be about giving this space to young people and just listening to them.

Being heard is one of the greatest gifts we can give and receive. People are always trying to do good, to help and to fix, but in my experience that doesn't help, what really helps is just being heard.

**For more information or to contact Jo
visit her website:**

**www.buildingbridgesforpeace.org**

### Sarah Clover, Action Transport Theatre, talks with Kevin Dyer, Writer and Joe Sumsion, Director 2006

**Sarah**: Kevin, why did you want to write the play?

**Kevin**: I was driving into Action Transport's office and I heard *Woman's Hour*. Jenny Murray was talking to Jo Berry. I heard her talk about how her dad was killed in the Brighton bomb and how she decided to meet the man who had planted the bomb, and she did, she went and met him.

Hearing her talk was inspiring. I wasn't thinking I've got to write this play, I just knew there was something in there I had to look at. It moved me, it was emotionally strong.

I came into the office and told Joe I'd just heard Jo on the radio, and I don't think I said it's a fantastic idea for a play, I hadn't got that far, but Joe said you've got to write that play.

**Joe**: I thought the story of Jo Berry and Pat Magee's meeting was remarkable, surprising, inherently dramatic. Two opposites choosing to come together, filled with meaning and interest.

Plays that include characters making hard choices and going to difficult places are often very dramatic, and I felt that this subject-matter would resonate with a 14+ audience. *Who am I? What do I want to become? What are the barriers and obstacles keeping me from fulfilling my potential?* Those kinds of questions are within Pat and Jo's story and they are also relevant for our audience.

**Kevin**: It is fantastic when you tell someone you have an idea for a play and they say, 'OK, I'm going to commission you to do it'. That's a great feeling, a joy. Because Action Transport is a company I work for, I've been able to test and share the play with colleagues and all the young writers connected to the company as well, all the way down the line.

**Sarah**: Kevin, how did you involve Jo Berry and Pat Magee?

**Kevin**: I knew that this was a play that needed research. I had to use facts. Sometimes with a play you don't, you use your own experience, or you make it all up. I knew this wasn't one of those.

I found out that on the 20th anniversary of the bombing in Brighton, Jo and Pat were going to meet again and run an open event. So on that day, 20 years after the bomb, I went to London and I just sat in the audience and I listened to Jo speak, and I listened to Pat speak. I then contacted Jo, she was the starting point for me because of *Woman's Hour,* and once I had spoken to her about the events, and also her life, I had to speak to Pat. I went to Belfast and met Pat Magee and did the same with him, talked, chatted about 20 years ago and now.

I couldn't write the play without hearing what they had to say, it wouldn't have been right. It would be like stealing their souls.

I knew that what had happened was a very personal thing for them. I knew that I could only write the play with their consent. I knew that it was their story, it wasn't my story, their lives, not my life, and I had to treat it with respect. So I wanted to explain to them why I wanted to write it and who was going to see it.

Obviously a lot of information is in the public domain about what happened 20 years ago. So I could read all that. I soon understood that their own lives and their own work, is connected with peace and with changing the world. I thought that Jo talking to me would help me write a play but also I knew that Jo was talking to the world and that maybe the play could help her, and maybe help Pat as well. I thought that in some way the play might pay them back.

**Sarah**: From talking to Jo she felt instinctively comfortable talking with you.

**Kevin**: There was no difficulty, I found that both Jo and Pat and their ideas were interesting, compelling. I enjoyed talking to them. One good thing about being a writer is that you get to talk to people different to yourself, fishermen, politicians, teachers, children, someone whose dad has been killed by a bomb and someone who's planted a bomb. It's an amazing job.

**Sarah**: Joe, how has it been working with Jo and Pat?

**Joe**: Jo and Pat, individually and together, work for peace. Part of their strategy is to promote their story and their experiences. That's not our agenda; we try to create brilliant plays which challenge and inspire our audiences.

With Jo and Pat it's complicated. All of the characters are fictional yet two of the characters bear many resemblances to real people. Steering a path through that complicated scenario has been challenging.

As commissioner, my job has been firstly to make sure that Kevin felt free to write an original work of art under no pressure from me or anybody else. At the same time the hope has been that Pat and Jo would want to continue their association with the play even though at no point would they or have they told us what to write. Practically that meant keeping them informed about the playmaking process. We've asked them at each draft for opinions (but not approval).

**Kevin**: Once I'd written the first draft my heart went faster when I knew that they were going to read it. Not because I wanted them to like it, but because I didn't want to betray them and their work and their lives. I only met Jo once after writing the first draft and moving on to the final draft, because I had to give myself the space to write the play. In the first draft Pat and Jo's own agendas were heavily in the play, and in the end I had to write the story. Something dramatic and interesting and captivating and surprising. And not worry about what Pat and Jo would think about it.

There's a truth in that all the characters in this play have to be truthful and do the things they would truthfully do. The whole researching process was important for me, about *Semtex*, bombs, checking into hotels, Blackpool, Brighton. I thought hard about what those places are really like. More importantly, it's getting what characters really feel and really say in situations, that's the important thing to do.

Personally, I've not been in the situations these characters have been in. I never really asked Pat and Jo to relive for me what those times were like. I had to dig deep into myself. I found it useful to write the play, come back to it a month later, write a bit more, and then come back to it a month later, and so on.

**Sarah**: Kevin, was it difficult deciding not to depict Jo and Pat directly in the play?

**Kevin**: In some ways it's been very easy because the story of it is so compelling. Sometimes when you write a play you are trying to make something out of nothing. There's something very emotional and powerful and far-reaching at the heart of this story. It's a playwright's gift.

What's real and not real is interesting. Some of the lines are Pat's lines, some are Jo's lines. But the characters are not Pat and not Jo. There's a common root, but it's about me, or the young writers I work with, about my dad, my own family. It definitely isn't Jo and Pat. Marnie is definitely, definitely not from Jo's family. I was very careful not to talk to Jo's family. That's one reason why the play isn't a documentary play about Jo and Pat, because it's also about how families work, and how when a bomb goes off it affects more than the person who was killed. I knew I wanted to talk about more than a man who planted a bomb, and the woman who had survived it. I had to move away from Pat and Jo otherwise I would be dragging in their families, and that's not fair on anybody.

**Joe**: And families are important in the play. For me it is a play about three central characters who all, to a degree, have life-changing experiences in their late teens/early twenties. All three central characters connect to the audiences who are, or have been, teenagers.

**Kevin**: Partly the play began because I was interested, and have been for some time, in what you do with those people that try and smash your life up. We are all in a situation sometimes when we come up against people who behave unreasonably. People who are unfair, aggressive, violent sometimes. What do you do and how do you respond when someone is abusing you? When your life is threatened by violence? Do you turn the other cheek or do you seek an eye for an eye? So when I heard Jo's story on the radio, and in some ways Pat's story, as part of a community being unfairly treated by the British, it just chimed in with me at the time.

**Joe**: Another reason why I programmed *The Bomb* is that the notion of what you would die for is particularly reson-ant for young people. I think many young people have a particular interest in suicide bombers, for instance, not least because many suicide bombers seem to be young themselves. *What would you die for?* And in the play – *what would you kill for?* These are questions that are particularly of interest to many teenagers.

I think it is about the development and articulation of your own personal morality. I think, broadly speaking, that young people are disengaged from conventional politics, many believe politicians are untrustworthy, but that does not mean young people are not themselves political, or that their own morality is not important. In a way this play is going to really question what people believe is right. It is a play of ideas.

**Sarah**: Many audiences or readers will respond by having been touched in some way by current terrorism, or as you say, Kevin, by any number of personal situations. How would you like readers or audiences to respond to the play?

**Kevin**: They will see things they haven't seen before. Some people will see things in a different way. When I started writing the play I thought about terrorism, forgiveness, Northern Ireland, Al Quaida; I had to go through that, get it out of the way, and then write the story about people, a mum and a daughter going away to Blackpool. And then something happens and they can't go. That's what it's about, a mum and her daughter, a woman who has to go and meet a man who has done something horrible to her and a man who goes to meet a woman in a very difficult meeting. Very simple human things. That's what happens to people and families all the time, so as I've written it more and more I've not thought about big stuff, just people I know.

**Joe**: As Director, I want the play to be moving and exciting without being titillating. It should be challenging for the audience. They should find it easy to step into the shoes of different characters. In that respect the play is challenging because it asks audiences to imagine – imagine you were making a bomb designed to kill people, imagine if your father was blown up, imagine your mother lives in the past and stops you living your own life.

**Kevin**: There is no message to the play. It does not say terrorism is good or bad, forgiveness is good or bad. When people watch the play some of them will connect with the characters they see before them. I would like to think they get involved with the emotional complexity of the situation. That they see themselves in one, two, three, four of the characters. Good plays allow you to explore dangerous things safely. Especially for younger people, they can see things in front of them that help them work out the world a bit, themselves a little bit. It is a play where the political and the personal come together. People respond personally and emotionally, rather than have to analyse anything about terrorism or Belfast or the British government. I think they'll laugh a bit, have a good time.

**Sarah**: What are you looking forward to producing on stage, Joe?

**Joe**: The biggest strength of *The Bomb* is that for three-quarters of the play it's like being inside Elizabeth's head. The play is written in a way that deliberately blends reality, memory, fantasy, imagination.

Alison Heffernan, the Designer, and I have found the design of this play challenging. But what we've tried to do, working in tandem with Julian Ronnie, the Composer, is to come up with a design which quite radically externalises the internal world of Elizabeth. One of the things we are trying physically and visually to show is the confusion and the chaos inside a particular character's head.

**Sarah**: Kevin, what are you most pleased with?

**Kevin**: I don't think writers are pleased until it's out, until people are putting their hands together at the end of the play.

I've loved writing it. It's weird being a writer, an artist, because your work does reflect you, it does change you.

You come out at the end of it a different person, just like in the play when Ned and Elizabeth meet and at the end of the meeting they are different people. I enjoy going into places and coming out a different person, like going through a tunnel.

The idea that you can go and talk to somebody who killed your dad with a bomb, is a great thing to do. Most people in the world don't talk to a brother, or a sister, or someone else for stupid little reasons. But you ask people why and they can't remember anymore. So for both characters in my play, and the people who started it all off, Jo and Pat, to talk to people on the other side is a truly great thing.

# THE BOMB

## Kevin Dyer

CHARACTERS:

**ELIZABETH**   She is trying to sort out what happened to her and her dad over twenty years ago. It has remained an under-current in her life ever since.

**MARNIE**   Elizabeth's daughter. Bright, modern girl. Just done her A levels, and desperate for a get-away-from-it-all break.

**NED KEENAN**   Political, intelligent with a sharp humour. The man who made and planted the bomb that killed Elizabeth's dad.

**LIZZIE**   Young Elizabeth. Has just left school and is going to go to India with friends.

**WILLIAM TOWNSHEND MP**   Elizabeth's father. Conservative Member of Parliament. At a critical point in his life. He has worked and been a man for the party all his working life. Now he is seeing his 'little girl' grow up and leave. Fun, clever.

**WOMAN** (on the ferry) A fortune-teller – a woman who sees beyond the outer shell of people.

**CHAMBERMAID** (Voice off only)


SET

*The rubble after the bomb went off. Even though the script is broken into scenes, there are no blackouts. Events that happen at different times and in different places are sometimes played simultaneously.*

## SCENE ONE

*Elizabeth's house. Friday 8.30am.*
*School is over and Elizabeth and Marnie are going to*
*Blackpool for a 'get-away-from-it-all' weekend.*
*Elizabeth is packed and ready to go. Marnie has*
*overslept and is packing in a chaotic hurry. A couple of*
*half packed suitcases and a rucksack.*

**MARNIE** *(Entering, eating breakfast cereal from a bowl*
*and getting dressed at the same time. She shouts*
*off:)* Why didn't you wake me?

**ELIZABETH** *(Off)* I did.

**MARNIE**          Did not!

**ELIZABETH** *(Off)* I did.

**MARNIE**          Christ! Where is it?

*She goes to run off.*

**ELIZABETH** *(Entering)* What now?

**MARNIE**          I've not got me razor. Shit.

**ELIZABETH**     Language. *(Doing up her bag, as Marnie*
*searches for the razor)* You should have done your
packing last night.

**MARNIE**          I was out.

**ELIZABETH**     Taxi'll be here any minute.

**MARNIE**          I know.

**ELIZABETH**     Cheese sandwiches and I'm making
vegetable soup. Is that all right?

**MARNIE**          Look at my legs. I'm a cave-woman.

**ELIZABETH**     It doesn't matter.

**MARNIE**  Not to you, but what about all those blokes in Blackpool. Poor things, waiting there, all their sad, deprived lives. *(Finds her razor.)* Goddit. Hold on boys, I'm on my way!

**ELIZABETH**  Will you get a move on?

**MARNIE**  I am. *(Packing tops and socks and a towel and a make-up case and toiletries)* What have I forgot?

**ELIZABETH**  You're wearing odd pumps.

**MARNIE**  Toss.

**ELIZABETH**  Language.

**MARNIE** *(As she changes them)* That milk was off. *(She sticks some toothpaste on her finger and quickly rubs at her teeth and tongue.)*

**ELIZABETH**  I'm going to walk the entire length of the beach, and when I get to the far end, ride back on a tram, and look at the lights.

**MARNIE**  I'm not sitting on a tram with a bunch of grannies.

**ELIZABETH**  I'll go on my own then.

**MARNIE**  Yeh, and get picked up by the local weirdo.

**ELIZABETH**  No.

**MARNIE**  Tramps, jehovahs, them people with pictures of rabbits, they love you, you're a weirdo magnet.

**ELIZABETH**  Excuse me.

**MARNIE**  And when I turn my back you'll be talking about the environment with some bloke in a cardigan.

**ELIZABETH**  Will not.

**MARNIE** *(Holding up a short skirt)* Shall I take this?

**ELIZABETH**     Marnie, that is not a skirt. That is a fat belt. Get a move on.

**MARNIE**     You seen me jeans?

**ELIZABETH**     They're on your legs.

**MARNIE**     Not these.

**ELIZABETH**     Your pale ones are in the wash, the skinny ones are on the kitchen radiator, the ripped ones are screwed up under your bed. It's only two nights. All you need is one change of clothes, toothbrush, spare socks, spare pants...

**MARNIE**     We're going to Blackpool, who needs pants? And as soon as we get there, we're in the sea...

**ELIZABETH**     I haven't got a cossie.

**MARNIE**     We'll go skinny-dipping.

**ELIZABETH**     I'm not –

**MARNIE**     Mum, joke. But what's the point of going if we don't have a laugh?

**ELIZABETH**     All right, we will do things, go to a disco –

**MARNIE**     Club.

**ELIZABETH**     Have a bop.

**MARNIE**     Dance.

**ELIZABETH**     Have a nice time.

**MARNIE**     I don't do nice.

**ELIZABETH**     I will let my hair down... and dance and drink and look at boys half my age, but you have to promise not to go off and leave me standing on my own like a lemon.

**MARNIE**     I promise. I won't leave you.

*Marnie has found some jeans, closed her bag and they've dragged them into a pile by the door. They sit on them, happy, ready, still.*

**MARNIE**     Do you know, more girls lose their
  virginity in Blackpool than any other town in Britain.
**ELIZABETH**     If you wanted to go wild, you should have
  gone with your friends, not your mum.
**MARNIE**     I'm teasing. And I know you did things
  when you were young, before the dinosaurs. You've
  just got out the habit. Me and you, we'll destroy
  Blackpool.
**ELIZABETH**     They don't know what is going to hit them.
**MARNIE**     Mum, this is, you know, great. Going with
  you. *(Elizabeth smiles.)* I feel like, sounds silly, that...
  I've grown up.
**ELIZABETH** *(Fondly at her)* You have... Now, have you
  been to the toilet?

*They laugh then the phone rings.*

**ELIZABETH**     Hold on.
**MARNIE**     It's the B & B saying they've double booked
  our room with a rugby team from Leeds.
**ELIZABETH** *(On the phone)* Hello ...
  Yes?
  Oh ...

*She sits down.*

**MARNIE**     Everything all right?

*Elizabeth waves at Marnie to be quiet.*

**ELIZABETH**    Yes.
  Well I was just going to...
  Yes. I do.
  It's just that...
  No... Course I can.
  No, no, let me get a pen.
  *(She signs at Marnie to pass her a pen. Marnie passes her one. She scribbles stuff down.)*
  Yes, I've got it. I'll be there...
  3 pm ferry from Holyhead. Then be at the house by 8.
  Thank you.
  Yes, I'll find it.
  Bye.... Bye.

*A noise. Elizabeth can hear it in her head. The noise, which we can't recognise, builds...*

**MARNIE**      Who was that?
**ELIZABETH**   My hands are shaking. Look at them. I...

*The noise still builds. Ned walks in – although he is in a different space and a different time. He carries two cases and a holdall.*

**MARNIE**      Who was it? Everything all right?
**ELIZABETH**   Yes... I think I'm going to be...

*She runs off to be sick.*

**MARNIE** *(Following her)* Mum..?

## SCENE TWO

*Grand Hotel, Brighton, 1984. 11.45am.*
*Ned is standing in Reception at the hotel. He is dressed*
*in a suit. He speaks in a very clear English accent.*

**NED**          Hello. Do you have a room for tonight?
Just me. A room on the front if possible.
Fine. Thank you.
Mills. Jeremy Mills.
Sign the register. Not too neat, not too squiggly. Read
name badge of girl on reception. Be normal. Friendly.
*(He smiles.)*
No thanks, Tanya, I'll carry them myself.


*He picks up his bags but does not exit.*


## SCENE THREE

*Elizabeth's house. Friday, 8.40am.*
*(Ned is still visible, as if standing at Reception in the*
*hotel)*
*Elizabeth re-enters, followed by Marnie. They are*
*midway through the argument.*


| | |
|---|---|
| **MARNIE** | But I've saved up. |
| **ELIZABETH** | I know. |
| **MARNIE** | And I've been looking forward to it. |
| **ELIZABETH** | All right. |
| **MARNIE** | End of exams treat, end of school – you |

promised.

**ELIZABETH**    All right, but you heard me. I've said. I've
got to go, the ferry's at 3, I've got to be there by 8.
I'm sorry. It's important.

**MARNIE**   Thanks.

**ELIZABETH**   I don't mean you're not.

**MARNIE**   But not as important as *him*.

**ELIZABETH**   Course you are. What can I do?

**MARNIE**   Don't go.

**ELIZABETH**   I've said now, you heard me, and Blackpool will still be there next week.

**MARNIE**   Phone him back.

**ELIZABETH**   It was someone else arranging it for him.

**MARNIE**   Well, phone them back and tell 'em.

**ELIZABETH**   I didn't take a number.

**MARNIE**   I'll get it.

*Marnie checks on the phone, dialling 1471.*

**ELIZABETH**   I've got to go. You and me we'll go to Blackpool on Monday.

**MARNIE**   I don't want to go Monday... Withheld number. Prats. The bags are packed. What do you want? A bloody good time –

**ELIZABETH**   Marnie!

**MARNIE**   Or meet him and rake it all up again? More weeping and crying and re-living it all over again. Like you always do.

**ELIZABETH**   No I don't.

**MARNIE**   Christ, Mum, what is going on in your head? Let's go to Blackpool and get pissed.

**ELIZABETH**   Please. I won't tell you again.

*They have reached an impasse. Marnie opens her sandwiches.*

**ELIZABETH**    They were for the trip.
**MARNIE**    What trip?

*She grabs a tube of ketchup and squeezes a long line onto the sandwich.*

**ELIZABETH**    That *is* disgusting.
**MARNIE**    Don't talk to me about disgusting. He was in the papers... for killing Grandad. Sick.
And you're gonna shake his hand.

*She bites into the sandwich, an angry, destructive gesture.*

**ELIZABETH**    Don't... You don't understand
**MARNIE**    Course not. Bimbo understand nothing.
*(Beat)* Why did he ring now?
**ELIZABETH**    Because he wants to meet me.
**MARNIE**    You don't have to go.
**ELIZABETH**    He wants to meet me.
**MARNIE**    And you jump at it. Like a, like a, I dunno. We were going away.
**ELIZABETH**    But now we're not. Sorry.

*Marnie's disappointment and frustration boil over.*

**MARNIE**    Well thanks, thanks, thanks! I don't want to go anyway. *(She empties out the contents of her* *case all over the floor.)* You're a cow. A bloody cow. *(She throws stuff. It goes everywhere. A real tantrum.)* Selfish, soddin' bloody cow.

*She is really hurt. She turns her back on Elizabeth. Elizabeth does nothing, she is confused, thinks she is more in the wrong than her daughter. She looks at her watch, and she starts to pick up the stuff on the floor. They cannot talk to each other.*

*The doorbell goes. No one moves. The doorbell rings again.*

**MARNIE**      I'll get it.

**ELIZABETH**      Leave it.

*Marnie goes. Elizabeth picks through the stuff. She picks up two bits of something broken and holds them together. They just don't 'stick'.*

*Marnie comes back.*

**MARNIE**      It's some bloke selling hoovers. He wants to come in and do a demonstration thing. I said he could come in and clear up the mess.

**ELIZABETH**      Marnie, not now we don't want a –

**MARNIE**      It's the taxi, isn't it? I told him to hang on. Do you know if you say the word gullible slowly it sounds like 'cucumber'? Go, on, try it.

**ELIZABETH** *(Slowly)* Gulli... *(Realising she's been had)* Oh.

**MARNIE**    He'll wrap you round his finger. He'll lie and lie and you'll believe every word. Cos that's what you want. He'll say sorry –

**ELIZABETH**    No, he won't.

**MARNIE**    Ten quid he will.

**ELIZABETH**    He won't.

**MARNIE**    And then you'll cry, and look at him with puppy eyes, and he'll look sad, and you'll hug him, and he'll hug you, and then he'll tongue you –

**ELIZABETH**    Enough. Stop it. Stop it!

**MARNIE**    He's a psycho. He'll get you on yer own then he'll stab you.

**ELIZABETH**    Don't be stupid.

**MARNIE**    Why else does he want to meet you? He killed Grandad, why shouldn't he kill you? Eh? Take a gun, put it in your bag, when he comes through the door, waste him!

*Marnie starts to go.*

**ELIZABETH**    Where are you going?

**MARNIE**    Not Blackpool.

*Marnie goes upstairs.*
*Elizabeth, alone, angry, hurt. She is tidying, sorting, picking bits up, and trying to think. She rubs the side of her head then she fetches the hoover, sharply turns it on. The sounds of a hoover to begin with, but then it is the sound of something else. Smoke starts to fill the room and the sound grows and grows into a distorted, crashing sound – a bomb exploding, slowed down and*

*fragmented, then a building crumbling in slow motion.*

**ELIZABETH**　　Hell, the soup! I forgot the soup. Marnie!
Marnie!
*(No reply. The sound continues. Elizabeth is confused,
stuck. The smoke continues.)*
The soup! Turn off the soup!
*(Shouting over the noise)* All right. All right...
*(She claps her hands over her ears and kicks off the
hoover. The sound stops.)*
... I won't go. I won't go.

*She runs off to the kitchen to sort out the soup.*

**SCENE FOUR**

*Grand Hotel, Brighton, 1984. 11.47am.*

**NED**　　　　　Pick up bags. Across the lobby. Just a
businessman doing his job. Doing his damndest to do
his job. Not too quick. Not too slow. In the lift. Going
up. First floor, electrical goods and DIY; Second floor,
sportswear; Third, seasonal goods; Fourth, children's
toys; Fifth floor, women's lingerie. Joke. Turn left.
Along the corridor. Room 533. Key, lock, open. In the
room, 'Do Not Disturb' sign on the door. Close the
door...

*He stands with his back to the door. He breathes out,
slowly.*

**NED**　　　　　Lock the door.
*(Now in his own accent)* Heart going, bang bang bang.

Mouth like the bottom of a budgie cage. Bathroom. Drink. Have a wee. Wash my hands. Unpack.

*He unzips his suitcases. We see tools, wires, bits of equipment, bags of fertilizer. He's nervous, on edge.*

**SCENE FIVE**

*Elizabeth's house. Friday, 8.50am.*
*The taxi horn is blowing.*

**ELIZABETH** *(To the driver, off)* All right, all right. *(To Marnie)* Just throw it all in. And we'll re-iron it when we get there.

**MARNIE**          Good, I'm glad. Really glad.

**ELIZABETH**          And me.

*They hurry to get the stuff back in. Marnie finds a skimpy bit of underwear.*

**MARNIE**          These aren't mine.

**ELIZABETH**          Well you can't destroy Blackpool on your own can you? I need a break. Shall we go up the tower?

**MARNIE**          Only if there's a lift. And we'll go to the fair. I'm gonna scream my head off.

**ELIZABETH**          I once went on the waltzers, long time ago, before your dad, and one of the fellahs running it, you know, that spin you round — he jumped in with me.

**MARNIE**          Was he good looking?

**ELIZABETH**   Can't remember. But he had a white shirt with all his buttons undone and a tattoo of an enormous snake.

**MARNIE**   Yo!

**ELIZABETH**   It went from his chest, all the way round, down past his belly button and the tail was, you know, somewhere down there.

**MARNIE**   Did you get off with him?

**ELIZABETH**   I did not. Always too chicken to do anything, me.

*Marnie laughs. All the stuff is re-packed.*

**MARNIE**   How long's it been going on?

**ELIZABETH**   It's not an affair, and I just had the call, you heard.

**MARNIE**   How long have you been writing to thingie then?

**ELIZABETH**   I haven't been writing to him. I just spoke to some people who know him and they arranged it … I did want to write, when he was in prison, but I couldn't do it, it was too hard.

**MARNIE**   Easy, I'd've thought. 'Dear… ' What's his name?

**ELIZABETH**   Ned Keenan.

**MARNIE**   Dear Mister Keenan … I hate you an' I'm gonna stick a bomb up your arse.

*Marnie zips her case.*

**ELIZABETH**   It's been in my head for years. Wanting to meet him. Couldn't get it out.

**MARNIE**   Like a fantasy like. Can't you think of blokes an' nice shoes like someone normal?

**ELIZABETH**   I am normal. Only it churns round in my head. My dad, the way he was killed, everything, all the time. I want it sorted out, that's all. Please, don't be angry.

*The taxi horn goes.*

**MARNIE** *(Picking up her bag)* Let's go then. To Blackpool and beyond...!

**ELIZABETH** *(Troubled)* I'll catch you up.

**MARNIE** *(Stops)* What now?

*They do not leave.*

**SCENE SIX**

*Grand Hotel, Brighton, 1984. 11.50am.*
*Ned turns on the table-lamp and sets up a 'workspace'.*

**NED**   Good-looking, that girl on reception. Very good-looking. 'Tanya'... Room 533, bang in the front of the hotel, sea-view. Dead posh. The cost of a beer here – it's not real. An' a bowl of soup costs an arm and a leg, an' if ash falls off your fag a porter catches it on a silver tray before it hits the ground. True. Well, nearly. *(Pause.)* And summat else, this is the detonator. For the bomb. True.

**ELIZABETH** *(To Marnie)* Sorry.

**NED** *(Making sure nothing is lying around.)* Time for a
quick piss.

*He goes to the bathroom.*

## SCENE SEVEN

*Elizabeth's house. Friday, 8.52am.*
*Marnie kicks a bit of furniture, then kicks it again and
again and again and again.*

**ELIZABETH** *(Firmly)* Stop it!

*Marnie stops. Looks at her Mum. They stand as if in the
rubble of their lives.*

**ELIZABETH**      I want to go to Blackpool. With you, now.
But I'm going to meet him, to stop it all, so it doesn't
carry on.

**MARNIE**      But this is 'carrying on'! Don't you get it?
You're keeping it going.

**ELIZABETH**      I'm trying to finish it, close it.

**MARNIE**      Rubbish. It's dead an' buried but you've
been digging it up and dragging it round with ya for
years. Mum – therapists, doctors, sleeping pills, hippy
rubbish – it gets in the way, it drove dad away.

**ELIZABETH**      Did not.

**MARNIE**      Did. It's like all that other stuff is in the
room with us all the time.

**ELIZABETH**      Stop it.

**MARNIE**        Or it's like living with a woman who's drownin' or something. I finished my exams and you said let's go away for a bit. It was like you were coming up for air. Alleluia. And now you're going under again. Up, down, up, down, always, we don't know whether we are coming or going.

**ELIZABETH**     This will help me, I don't know, dump it.

**MARNIE**        On me! Don't go, Mum, promise you won't see him. He's a murderer. People died. Grandad died.

**ELIZABETH**     I have to go see him.

**MARNIE**        Go on then. Go. Have a cosy chat with him, get it off your chest. Cough it all up... Only if you go, I'm not waiting here like a Muppet. I won't be here when you get back. If you don't want to do Blackpool, that's fine. Room's booked, I'm going anyway. And then I've got Uni' in September so that's it. *Adios amigo.* You go back I'll go forward. Is that what you want?

**ELIZABETH**     No.

**MARNIE**        Blackpool it is then. *(Beat)* Meeting him won't change anything.

**ELIZABETH**     If I don't then I'm stuck, aren't I — a victim, forever.

**MARNIE**        For god's sake, just get over it.

**ELIZABETH**     I want to hear why he did it, that's all. Then I can —

**MARNIE**        Cool. But I won't be here when you get back.

*Taxi horn.*

**MARNIE**        I'll go on my own then. I'll tell 'em at the
        Bed and Breakfast that you're dead. That you died
        years ago. I'll tell them that I've been making it up that
        I've got a real mother.

*Marnie goes out with her case.*

*Elizabeth tries to pick up her rucksack, but can't lift it.
The noise builds up, and up and up and up, till it is
deafening her. She is confused, unable to act. Her palms
are sweating, her hands are shaking. She is frightened.*

**ELIZABETH**     Daddy!?

*Enter Lizzie. She is Elizabeth, 1984.*

**ELIZABETH**     He sent a car to pick me up.
**LIZZIE**        A car to Brighton.

*Lizzie takes Elizabeth's bag.*
*Elizabeth does not watch; she more internally re-lives it,
reacting to it.*

**LIZZIE**        Big hotel, by the sea.
        Through the doors, straight past reception, across the
        lobby. The lift doors are closing, so I run, run and just
        manage to squeeze in.
**ELIZABETH**     There are two big men, with suits on and
        guns under their jackets. They look me up and down.
**LIZZIE**        And there's a woman – blue suit, big hand-
        bag, hard hair. Margaret Thatcher. Get this. I'm in the

lift with the Prime Minister. *(She giggles.)* And she says, 'What the hell are you doing in my lift?'

**ELIZABETH**     No, she says, 'How very good to see you.' She has a soft face, blue eyes.

**LIZZIE**     I nearly curtsy. What a prat.

*William enters. He laughs and shoots her like a cowboy, firing arrows and hollering like a Red Indian. Lizzie shoots back. Elizabeth enjoys this. He gets hit by an imaginary arrow.*

**WILLIAM**     Lizzie Poppet!

**LIZZIE**     Daddy!

*They hug.*

**WILLIAM**     Your mother tells me you're off tomorrow.

**LIZZIE**     Yes.

**WILLIAM**     Off your rocker more like. *(Pretending not to know.)* Where is it you're going?

**LIZZIE**     India.

**WILLIAM**     Long way to go for a curry. So... *(As if he knows nothing about her coming here to see him.)* ... what brings you here?

**LIZZIE**     Very funny, you know why, and you're lucky to see me at all because I have to be up at five to catch a plane.

**WILLIAM**     You'll have to run jolly fast... to catch a plane.

**LIZZIE**     So, have you booked me a nice room for tonight?

**WILLIAM**       Sorry, darling, party conference. Chokka. No room at the inn. Joseph and Mary are in sleeping bags in the car park.

**LIZZIE**       What then?

**WILLIAM**       I had thought dinner...

**LIZZIE**       Fab.

**WILLIAM**       ...but Maggie's on the warpath.

**LIZZIE**       I saw her in the lift, she seemed all right to me.

**WILLIAM**       She's called everyone to dinner at 8. And we men in grey suits have got to be there, no excuses.

**LIZZIE** *(Disappointed)* Oh...

**WILLIAM**       So it's a quick chat, bit of a hug and the car will take you back.

**LIZZIE**       No wonder Mummy hates you.

**WILLIAM**       Does she?

**LIZZIE**       Not as much as me.

**WILLIAM**       Not as much as *I*. *(Re: her rucksack)* What the hell is that? Where are you going? Climbing Snowdon, with the Brownies?

**LIZZIE**       India. Travelling. Tomorrow. *(He looks blank.)* Stop being such a – you know all about it!

**WILLIAM** *(Getting out his wallet)* Here you are then. *(Lizzie says nothing. She doesn't want paying off.)* Come on, my little chick is leaving the nest. I'm coughing up for the last time...
Will you be doing voluntary work and stuff? In India? *(She nods.)*
You can't give to the poor if you've nothing yourself. *(He puts the money on the table.)*

**LIZZIE**       I think you have three minutes till you have to go and suck up to the Prime Minister.

**WILLIAM** *(Looks at his watch)* True... Poppet, listen, I'll be three seats from Maggie – with the home secretary on my left, and a cousin of the Queen on my right. Tonight I can do anything; I could change the date of Christmas if I bloody well wanted... If I have a little wordy-word, I could get you a research job in the party, something in the palace even.

**LIZZIE** I can't. Bombay. There's a gang of us going.

**WILLIAM** I get it. I give up everything for the party, you give up everything to go to a party?

*He laughs at this.*

**LIZZIE** Dad – school, exams, I've finished. I'm going.

**WILLIAM** India... the final frontier... And bad dad trapped in his suit, a rat running round a wheel. All right, go. Advice: don't do drugs and don't sleep around.

*She raises her eyebrow, as if to say, 'Too late, daddy-o.'*

**LIZZIE** Why'd you send for me?

**WILLIAM** Wanted to see you – before you trek off and catch some foreign disease and I have to pay to fly you home. *(Silence.)* All right, Little Miss Stubborn. Advice two: if you're in deep water, and somebody offers to help, let them pull you out.
*(Pause. He gently puts the money in her bag. She is sad that she's come here just for this.)*

We came here once before when you were this high.
*(He indicates.)*

**LIZZIE**          Bet you were working?

**WILLIAM**          Holiday. You had a strop on then. There
was a little rasher of sand between the stones and the
sea, and you had a new bucket and spade and wanted
to build a sandcastle. The sun came out. 'Swimmy
time,' I said. 'Want build castle,' you said. 'Learn swim
first,' I said, 'then sandcastle.' You stuck your lip out.
*(Lizzie notices she has her lip stuck out. She pulls it
back.)* A determined little dot in a swimming costume.

**LIZZIE**          Haven't you got to rush off and lick
Maggie's –?

**WILLIAM**          Two minutes, don't rush me. I dragged you
out there to the salty sea, held your tummy and you
kicked and kicked and splashed.

*Elizabeth and Lizzie both nod.*

**WILLIAM**          'Good girl' I shouted. My legs were blue,
it was freezing. 'Kick kick kick! Go on, go on!'
You wanted so badly to get away from me, even then,
to swim out of my arms and away. Lip out, kick, kick,
splash, splash... and then... *(He imagines her, watches
her, swimming away from him. Elizabeth moves her
arms, swimming, reliving it.)* One of the greatest
achievements of my life. Better than being an MP,
better than tea with the Duke of Edinburgh's missus. I
bought you a little flag for your sandcastle, as a
reward, and... *(He gestures, living the moment, as if
offering the flags to her.)* ... you didn't want it, you
wouldn't touch it.

You went off and played with a plastic cup and some old lolly stick... Lizzie...

**LIZZIE**  Don't.

**WILLIAM** *(Truthfully)* Cheerio.
*(He leans to kiss her but she is stone. It is Elizabeth who closes her eyes as if to receive the kiss.)*
My little... not a little girl anymore, going away.
*(Sighs)* Is Daddy that grotesque?

**LIZZIE**  One minute left.


*He holds out his hand. She shakes it. She turns to go.*


**WILLIAM**  Wait... *(She turns back.)*... Margaret Thatcher can bloody well wait.
*(He goes to her and holds her.)*
You are the most beautiful thing.
Go on! Go away! Party! And I'll give it all up,
I promise. This is my last conference, finito, definite, and when you come back we'll...

**LIZZIE**  What?

**WILLIAM**  I dunno... build a sandcastle?

**LIZZIE** *(Content)* All right.

**ELIZABETH** *(Content)* All right. And I'll put the flags on, one in each corner. *(Elizabeth is smiling.)*

**WILLIAM**  Now... don't get pregnant – kids ruin your life. *(He laughs. He holds her tight.)*
On my gravestone let it be writ, 'I did not spend enough time with my little girl. She is stroppy and a pain in the backside but she has the face of an angel and I miss her more than...'

**LIZZIE**  What?

**WILLIAM** *(Collecting some notes and running out)*
Order something from Room Service. Whatever  you want. Why don't you stay? Yes, you have the bed, I'll sleep in the bath. Maybe not. Close the door behind you, Pops.

*He's gone. Lizzie looks around the room. She is happy. She runs her finger over the furniture. Elizabeth is troubled. Lizzie goes, giving Elizabeth the rucksack on the way. Elizabeth hugs the bag.*

**ELIZABETH**     Along the corridor, wait for lift, then down, reception, out, cross the road... and look at the sea. How wide and far it is. And the car came to take me. And that was it.

*Marnie enters.*

**MARNIE**     Mum. Tell him he's a bad man for killing Grandad. Tell him he's a bad man.

*She goes. Elizabeth stays.*

**SCENE EIGHT**
*Grand Hotel, Brighton, 1984. 12.30am.*
*He comes back in. He works on building the bomb, putting all the bits on the table. After a while he says...*

**NED**     This is the battery. And this bit of wire connects it to the detonator. So the battery comes on, the current goes along this wire, and when it gets to here the detonator goes crack! Like a skull hitting the pavement. Crack.

*(As he strips the outer layer off some cable)* Came
here when I was a kid, with me mam and dad. Didn't
stay in this hotel, no way: some poxy campsite six
miles from the beach, up to our arses in mud.

Doing this, it's not rocket science, but it's not sucking
no lollipop neither.

Tanya. I knew a Tanya once. Tanya Willetts. Best
looking girl in primary school. Had a beauty spot, so
she said, but wouldn't tell anyone exactly where it was.
We lived near the canal and the big kids used it as a
weapon of terror, one day they grabbed me, held me
by me ankles from the lock gates over the water. They
said if I didn't do what they wanted they'd drop me.
Tanya Willetts was with 'em. The canal below my head
was like a sheet of black steel. Sheer sides of the lock,
and the water below me twenty feet deep.

Blood was filling my head, and my mam's voice, 'Don't
ruin those jeans, don't dirty that jumper'. Tanya
Willetts was staring at me, laughing. Even when I was
lookin' at her from upside down she was gorgeous.
She was laughing at me and I fell out of love there
and then. Hanging from my ankles I thought if a stone
fell in this lock it'd never come up, not for a million
years.

But I am no stone. 'Drop me,' I said. 'Go on, drop me.'
They stopped laughing. If they pulled me up they'd be
the chickens wouldn't they?

So they let go. Down I went through the black into
blacker black.

Tanya was shouting, 'Ned! Ned!' I liked that. I couldn't
hear her, cos' I was under the surface, but I could see
up through the water; her mouth opening and closing
like a fish. I stayed under, looking up through the
water. I waited. And waited. Should've seen their faces.

Then I came up, dead slow, eyes closed, as if I was a gonner. She was crying. If I'd asked her, she'd've shown me that beauty spot there and then.
I knew then, at that moment, I could do anything. Anything.

*He goes back to his work. Stony, determined, the sweat dripping off him.*

## SCENE NINE

*Elizabeth stands waiting, in the 'neutral house'. She waits and waits. She puts the bag down, puts on lipstick, her hand shaking. She holds herself, forcing herself to be calm. Enter Ned. They look at each other.*

**ELIZABETH**    I'm really pleased you've come.

**NED**    Thank you for inviting me.

**ELIZABETH**    And you me. It's a good place to meet, in a neutral house.

**NED**    How was your trip?

**ELIZABETH**    Fine.

**NED**    It didn't rain?

**ELIZABETH**    A little.
*(Then it all wells up inside her, screaming at him.)*
You...!

*We don't hear her say 'bastard' but that is what she says. Noise bursts in. A confusion of explosion, falling masonry, screams, calls for help, police sirens, ambulances, fire, news reports, etc etc. This noise continues under/over the rest of this scene.*
*She verbally launches herself at him. We only catch*

*fragments of what she says. They argue vehemently.*
*They say what they have wanted to say to 'the other side'*
*for the last 20 years. We hear just shards of the follow-*
*ing conversation.*

**ELIZABETH**     You've got a nerve to come here and stand
here after what you have done.

**NED**     Now hold on.

**ELIZABETH**     You are a murderer! A murderer!

**NED**     Wait up! Just shut your mouth a minute.

**ELIZABETH**     You ruin people's lives and you don't
give a damn.

**NED**     Don't talk to me about ruining people's
lives. If you'd seen what I'd seen, you middle-class –

**ELIZABETH**     What?! What!

**NED**     What do you know? You know nothing.

**ELIZABETH**     And scum like you does, I suppose! You
come over here with your bombs and who the hell do
you think are, Mr IRA man?

**NED**     What choice do we have, eh? What choice?
To lie down and let your armoured cars run right over
us?

**ELIZABETH**     You're sick, sick in the head, sick in your
mind.

*At last, she picks up an object to strike him – it is a pair*
*of scissors from the debris they are standing in. He has*
*his backed turned, is walking away. She raises the*
*scissors but he turns, sees her. The noise dips and she*
*sees herself holding the weapon.*

**ELIZABETH** *(lowering them)* I'm sorry.
**NED**        No, I am. I am.

*Then Marnie's words come back to her.*

**ELIZABETH** *(Quietly)* She said you'd wrap me round your little finger. You'd lie and lie and I'd believe every word. You'd say sorry –
**NED**        Yes.
**ELIZABETH**      And then I'd cry, and look at you with puppy eyes, and you'd look sad.
**NED**        True.
**ELIZABETH**      And I'd hug you, and you'd hug me and... *(He reaches out for her, takes the scissors from her.)* It'd be great. We'd have a cosy chat, that's what she said, get if off my chest. Yeah cough it all up, I'd feel better, you'd feel better. Then, she said, all alone, you'd stab me.
**NED**        Too right. I can only take so much of your claptrap.

*He stabs her. She falls. She gets up.*

**ELIZABETH**      It'd be great. We'd have a cosy chat... I'd get it off my chest... cough it all up, feel better, feel better. Then you'd stab me.
**NED**        Too right.

*He stabs her. She falls. She gets up.*

**ELIZABETH**     Great. Cosy chat. Chest. Cough it up, feel
better, feel better.

**NED**     Too right. Too right.

*He stabs her, stabs her, stabs her.*
*He stands over the body.*
*She is dead. He has finished the job. He goes.*

**ELIZABETH** *(Getting up)* My daddy said. When he came
back... *(Soundtrack stops.)* ...when he came back
we'd...

*Ned isn't there.*

**ELIZABETH**     ...but he never did.

*She scrambles for the phone, picks it up. She's in a hurry.*

**ELIZABETH**     Yes... Hello, I'd like a cab to the station
please. No, straightaway. The train's at ten past and I
need to get to the ferry for –
Oh.
O...
Forget it then, forget it, I'll walk.

*She grabs her rucksack and rushes out.*

**SCENE TEN**
*Grand Hotel, Brighton, 1984. 2.30pm.*
*Ned is alone in room 533. It is still three and a half*

*weeks before the bomb goes off. He's installing the bomb,
taking bags of fertiliser from his cases.*

**NED** *(Taking off the bath panel)* It's a good hotel; no
    chewing gum on the carpets, no one upstairs banging
    away. My dad used to use gelignite – working in the
    building trade blasting rock for sewers and stuff, only
    the fumes off the gelignite gives you terrible head-
    aches. *(Packing fertilizer under the floor)* I got
    involved at the age of nineteen when I saw a small
    community being crapped on by the British. They had
    to respond; I had to help 'em.

*There is a knock on the door.*

**CHAMBERMAID** *(Voice off)* Chambermaid.
**NED** *(Changing his voice, suddenly scared, covering up
    the half-made bomb)* No. I'm fine. I'm fine thank you.
    It's fine, everything's fine.
    *(He waits for her to go. A long wait.)*
    Then soldiers were on the streets, picking us up, taking
    us back to their places. Bundled in the back of an
    armoured personnel carrier, chucked out, lined up...
    questions, bit of bother, you know, it was pretty rough.
    This is Semtex. *(He sniffs it like a fat Cuban cigar.)*
    The best. No headaches with this baby. Not for me
    anyway.

*He wires up the Semtex. He works with concentration.*

## SCENE ELEVEN

*On the deck of the ferry. 4.45 pm.*
*Elizabeth struggles out on to the top deck of the ferry.*
*She's wearing a coat. It is slashing down with rain. The*
*wind is howling. She's talking loudly into her mobile*
*phone. We do not hear the other end (Marnie) of the*
*conversation.*

**ELIZABETH**　　　Have you arrived yet? Where are you?
　　Are you at the B and B ...?
　　Because I'm worried ... Good ...
　　No, I'm on my way there. I came up on deck for a bit of
　　fresh air. I had to get away from some woman...
　　I don't know, just sort of, looking at me. Had a hat on
　　like a pudding...
　　No, not her, her hat ...
　　I'm not ...
　　I am not ...
　　I am *not* a weirdo magnet ...
　　Marnie, listen, I just wanted to tell you...

*Sound of the ferry hooter. The woman with the hat*
*enters at a bit of a distance.*

**ELIZABETH**　　　I can't turn back now, how can I?...
　　Don't be so ... Hold on, the woman's here ...
　　The woman with the ...
　　Never mind.
**WOMAN** *(Walking past, to Elizabeth)* Evening.
**ELIZABETH** *(Turning away from the woman. To Marnie)*
　　Go to the B and B, check in, then ...
　　I can't, I can't ...
　　Are you in Blackpool? ...

Well I can hear you. Marnie, I'll be back in the morning. Love you. *(Marnie hangs up.)* Damn you then.

*Elizabeth's hand is shaking, an involuntary action. She is distressed, alone. We hear the wind and rain and the sound of the ship's engine.*

*The woman comes across to her.*

**WOMAN**       Quite a crossing isn't it?

**ELIZABETH** *(Going)* Excuse me.

**WOMAN**       Bit of a journey? Below deck, there's no air, is there? And it stinks of chips.

**ELIZABETH**       If you want money –

**WOMAN**       Don't say you 'ent got none, cos it 'ent true, nobody travels with nothing. Not that I want any. I want nothing. But when someone's drownin' it's my right to give 'em a hand, isn'it?
*(Pause. Elizabeth's hand is still shaking.)*
Below deck, them people, as grey as the sea every one of 'em. But not you, girl. You're in Technicolor.

**ELIZABETH**       Sorry, I really am not interested.

**WOMAN**       I'm not the God squad.
*(The woman puts her hand on Elizabeth's. Holds it. Steadies it. Elizabeth stops stock-still. The woman turns the hand and looks at the palm.)*
You're meeting a man... an important man. *(With a laugh)* But they always think they're important, don't they?

**ELIZABETH**       Excuse me, I just need to pop to the toilet.

**WOMAN**       Don't mess around, girl – it's too late for messing around. *(She looks again at Elizabeth's hand.)*

**ELIZABETH**       I'm not a magnet.

**WOMAN**       No, you are flesh and blood. *(Looking at the hand)* Unfinished business. And you're going to finish it, eh? *(Elizabeth nods.)* Good. *(Holding the hand)* There's a man. A man. And a room, and in the room –

**ELIZABETH**       Is the man.

**WOMAN**       Who's doing this? *(She looks at the hand again, as if seeing a room there.)* In the room, is… a woman. You. The door knocks. And you let him in.

**ELIZABETH**       Does he hurt me?

*The woman looks at her.*

**WOMAN**       I think he already has, love.

*Elizabeth nods.*

**WOMAN**       There you are, the two of you. And here, here's someone else. Female. Girl. Fair –? *(Elizabeth shakes her head.)* Dark hair. Stroppy little madam.

**ELIZABETH**       Marnie. I don't know where she is.

**WOMAN**       She's by the sea. And she's doing… doesn't want you to know what she's doing.

**ELIZABETH**       I'm going back, I've got to. I'm cold.

**WOMAN**       You're boiling, girl, boiling over. There is no going back.

**ELIZABETH**       I've got to go back.

**WOMAN**          You're on a boat that goes from here to
there, and where's the future? There, there.

**ELIZABETH**          Is he a good man?

**WOMAN**          You are a good woman.

**ELIZABETH** *(Pulling her hand away)* You're not telling me
anything. Are you playing with me?

*She looks hard out at the horizon.*

**WOMAN**          It's good looking at the sea. Clears your
head. *(Elizabeth breathes out)* Go on, breathe, girl.
You've been holding your breath for too long.
*(Elizabeth breathes the sea air.)*
Go on!

**ELIZABETH**          I'm... I'm... *(scared)*

**WOMAN**          Who wouldn't be?

**ELIZABETH**          It's right isn't it? To go there?

**WOMAN**          Your shoulders, look at 'em. You've been
carrying it a long time.

**ELIZABETH** *(Straightening up)* What should I say to him?

**WOMAN**          You'll know. You're a bucketful of words,
you're brimming, right to the top. You've got more
words, girl, than water in the ocean.

**ELIZABETH**          When I close my eyes I can't see my
father's face any more. Can you?
*(The woman shakes her head. She holds Elizabeth's
hand, tight.)*

**WOMAN**          It's freezing, isn't it? Good job I got a hat.
Do you like my hat? Would you like it? Go on, you
have it.

**ELIZABETH**          No thank you.

**WOMAN**   You can have it if you want.

**ELIZABETH**   No, no please. Can I ask you something?

**WOMAN**   Course.

**ELIZABETH**   How's it all end?

**WOMAN**   You an optimist? *(Elizabeth nods.)*
 Pretty good then.

**ELIZABETH**   But sometimes a pessimist.

**WOMAN**   Not so good then.

**ELIZABETH**   I couldn't. *(Giving her the hat back.)*
 Thank you.

**WOMAN**   One last thing...

**ELIZABETH**   Yes?

**WOMAN**   Turn the tap on. Tell him hard.

**ELIZABETH**   Thank you.

*The woman goes.*

## SCENE TWELVE

*Grand Hotel, Brighton, 1984. 2.35pm.*

**NED** *(He runs through a mental check-list, touching each 'item' with his forefinger.)* Battery, check. Connector, check. Switch, yes. Timer, yes. Detonator. Semtex, check. Two booby traps wired up in parallel – micro-switch type, check. Arm the device. It doesn't tick. It's a tiny buzzing noise, like something sleeping. And in twenty-four days, in the middle of the night, when it's ready, the buzz gets louder, a tiny bit louder, then silence, for a count of three and then ...
*(He brushes at something on his face, he brushes again. Then he catches the money spider.)*

Y'all right little fellah? ...
If you're a little thing, a creepy-crawly caught in the
hands of a giant, he grabs you and holds you tight. *(He
closes his hands round the spider.)* There's no way out,
no way at all. Walls, floor, ceiling, all too strong. It's all
crushing you. *(He starts to close his hands on the
spider)* But you think and think and work and work and
eventually, eventually, crack, smash it all open and you
get free. *(He opens his hands, lets the spider go)* That's
a good feeling that is. *(To the spider)* Hey, Incey, bit of
advice... get outta here.

*He puts the spider well out of harm's way.*

## SCENE THIRTEEN

*Outside the Grand Hotel, Brighton, then inside the hotel
and Room 533, 1984. 7.45pm.*

*Marnie stands on the prom with her case. It is windy,
there are seagulls. We think she is in Blackpool. She
looks at the hotel. We see her decide: she walks through
a revolving door.*

**MARNIE**      Through the door. Marble floor.
Reception desk bigger than our house.
*(She continues to Reception.)*
Hello... I'd like a room, please.
No I haven't booked. Just for tonight, I think...
Just me, and I'd like a room on the front please... 'erm
could I have a particular room?
... 533.
Give card. Hand shaking. Feel hot. Man on reception
swipes it. I'm boiling. Take card.

No I can manage. Thank you.
Find the lift. In. Up. Floor Five. Left. Along the
corridor. Through the door then I'll get me breath
back... find out what all the bloody fuss is about. If she
knew I was here... she makes me want to puke my
guts. Use the card thingy. Open the door...

*She steps in. There is a noise, which gets louder. It is in
Marnie's head.*

**NED** Before you leave, scour the floor. Don't
leave anything. No clippings, bits of wire, nothing.
Leave a towel on the floor, complimentary dressing-
gown slung across the bed. Normal guest in a normal
room. Everything normal. Good day's work. It doesn't
tick: it's a tiny buzz, like something sleeping, and in
twenty-four days in the middle of the night, when it's
ready, the buzz of the timer gets louder, a little bit
louder. And then it stops. Then silence, for three
seconds. And then... *(He smiles, picks up his cases.)*
Lighter now.
Shame really, this hotel's got a nice pool, and I had no
time to use it.
Along the corridor.
In the lift. Down.
Ground floor.
Across the lobby. Terrible carpet, they should get rid of
it. Reception.
*(Back into 'good English')* I'd like to check out, please.
Jeremy Mills. Room 533.
Cash, please.
Yes, very comfortable, Tanya, thank you.
Goodbye.

*He smiles and goes.*
*Marnie, alone, stands there taking it all in.*

**MARNIE**      Oh Mum.

## SCENE FOURTEEN

*The neutral house. Nearly 8pm.*
*Also Room 533, in the hotel in Brighton at the same time.*

*Marnie, in room 533 is taking it all in.*

*Elizabeth, in Ireland, takes off her coat and waits.*

*Ned arrives. Twenty years or more have passed for him*
*since he left the hotel. His palms are sweating. He*
*adjusts his tie, clears his throat – all tiny delaying*
*tactics. They look at each other.*

**ELIZABETH**   I'm really pleased you've come.
**NED**         Thank you for inviting me.
**ELIZABETH**   And you me. It's a good place to meet, a
   neutral house.
**NED**         How was your trip?
**ELIZABETH**   Fine, no problems.
**NED**         It didn't rain.
**ELIZABETH**   A little.
**NED**         And the ferry was OK.
**ELIZABETH**   Yes, thank you. And you?
**NED**         Yes. Good

*They stand, opposite each other in the room. No words.*
*She gestures for him to sit. He does. So does she.*

**NED**          Who goes first? *(She shrugs.)* To start
then, I believe if you find a platform for explaining
things, you should take it. I am here because I feel
obliged to tell you what led someone like me to
participate in the action.
I got involved at 19, doing what I could to fight back,
redress the balance. On the streets, chucking stuff,
then more organised but it was like we had sticks
and you had armoured cars, night sights, the lot.
They'd sweep the area, pull us all in, again and again.
Those things change you. But it wasn't bitterness or
hate. I want to say that, it was political. Brighton
wasn't a result of getting beaten up in the back of an
army truck or nothing, it wasn't. Then I was 21 when I
was jailed for two years. With no trial. Banged up with
no trial. That changes you.
When I came out, I knew exactly what I was going to
do. I was getting out of jail to volunteer for active
service. If we want them to listen, we had to take the
war to the Government, to the heart of England.
I believe if you look back objectively you will see that
all avenues were closed to us, that our only recourse
was to engage in a violent conflict. No one 'uld talk to
us, see, the press weren't interested. The lies and the
lies about us. To be powerful there has to be someone
who isn't powerful, and your government were doing
their damndest to make us, me, unpowerful. And
there comes a point when you change, when you fight
back.

**ELIZABETH**     Did you know you were going to say all
that before you came?

**NED** *(Beat)* Sort of. I was told last Wednesday you wanted to meet me, and it's been going round my head ever since.

**ELIZABETH**      It's been going round my head ever since the bomb. Every day for more than twenty years I've tried to put it in a box and keep the lid on but it keeps... *(She gestures 'bursting out'.)* Brighton, the bomb, my father, meeting you.

**NED**              It was political. I knew what I was doing, yeah, it wasn't psychological, emotional, nothing of the kind, and Brighton, from our perspective, was a justified act. Your father was part of the political elite. Your father was a legitimate target. *(Elizabeth gasps.)* Violence arises out of weakness.

**ELIZABETH**      Yes?

**NED**              The British state has all the power and yet resorts to violence. That isn't right. If you have the power you don't abuse it. When you see some big dad, some fat mum smacking their kids in the supermarket. You don't do that. And people who have no power, forced into a corner, act violently.

**ELIZABETH** *(takes a deep breath, holds on)* I don't believe revenge or killing someone is the answer.

**NED**              We were in a war and a war results in casualties. I don't say that lightly. How could our community survive? How could we break out of the siege? On top of the flats, on the top, were army bases. Men were shot from the top of those flats, others by colluding forces, cars going past shooting people. Six people were shot in one night. You have to fight that. Elizabeth, Brighton worked. Because of Brighton, things changed. Like I can now sit down and talk to you here.

*He sits, the justification over, giving nothing away on his face.*

**ELIZABETH**     I looked at pictures of you, when you were sent to prison and gave that salute *(She clenches her fist.)* And when you came out, I looked for remorse, but there was none. *(Silence.)* Why?

**NED**     Because that is the only way we could be heard.

**ELIZABETH**     I was there the night before. My father asked me to stay over. It could have been me.

**NED**     I wish there'd been another way. There was none.

**ELIZABETH**     What about the innocent ones who died? The receptionist?

**NED**     My actions were legitimate.

**ELIZABETH**     She was a girl, working on the reception desk. A person with a name. How is that 'legitimate'?

**NED**     Sometimes people just have to defend themselves.

**ELIZABETH**     Against who? The chambermaid? Who's had nightmares ever since... can't work, her nerves shot to pieces?

**NED**     My mam slept in her clothes night after night for months, years, they all did, cos you never knew what was going off, if someone was gonna come walking into your room in the night with a gun. You cannot tell an oppressed person just to lie down and go to sleep.

**ELIZABETH**     There's always a reason, a reason they can kill more people. The bombs are still going off. When does that end?

**NED**            Weak people have to act –

**ELIZABETH**    I feel weak: and my daughter, whose
grandad she never saw because you – *(killed him)*, she
told me to put a gun in my bag. I feel weak: I can't
change it, I can't bring him back, I had no say in any of
it. So do I get the gun out my bag and kill you, kill you
dead? Should I? *(She puts her hand in her bag.)* I have
no gun. I need no gun. Or bomb…

**NED**            I understand why you have a difficulty
with my belief that violence cannot be ruled out and is
an effective political method.

**ELIZABETH**    Too right!! Because it's stupid and
pathetic!

**NED**            It was not the act of a madman, some
crazed bomber; there was a central code, a motivation
and logic behind it. Cold judgement. If that helps.

**ELIZABETH**    So, in that hotel it was all clear cut and
absolute. This needs to be done. One direction. Sounds
so easy.  There's a voice in my head that says, 'You
shouldn't be talking to the man who killed your father.'
Meeting you is hurting people – the families of other
people you have killed… my daughter, now *her* life is
*(she gestures 'being blown to bits')* Am I not making
more pain? When you were released from prison, I
thought 'You can walk free and my dad's dead. My
dad's dead.'

**NED**            Meeting you is a consequence; it's worse
than jail; it's a consequence I deserve, but I have to
weigh it. It's something I have to work through. I'm
going back over it now, making sense of it.

**ELIZABETH**    And me. I know violence happens when
the feeling you're not being heard gets too strong and
when bad things happen. Some people can just shut

the door on it and get on with their lives, but I'm really hurting, a lot today. Pain, the pain inside. The risk, here, is getting more hurt. Sitting here with the man who killed my father...

**NED** It's new this... you, me... like we are involved in some sort of experiment here...

**ELIZABETH** How dare you think my father was worth killing for what you wanted to do? How dare you?

**NED** I... I can't undo that. I...

**ELIZABETH** And wanting to become ... *(friends)* and build the bridge and understand. When you planted that bomb and it went off, the war, the conflict is now mine, and that's what I'm ... here now ... I'm fixing. I know what your struggle was. I know my dad was in the way.

**NED** You... *(He struggles for words.)* ...there's a wall *(between us)* ...but we can dismantle it.

**ELIZABETH** Can we? Can we? Not on my own we can't! ...I do understand, you know. Or am trying to, have been trying to for over twenty years, that you say you had no choice but to plant the bomb.

**NED** There were no avenues open.

**ELIZABETH** We all get angry, desperate, and want to smash and destroy and hurt and ... and I know, in my head. If I'd been in your situation... I'd have done the same. *(Beat)*
But he was my daddy.


*Ned takes off his glasses. She has had an effect on him. He wipes his eyes.*


**NED** When the bomb went off...

**ELIZABETH**    My life changed forever. I changed.
**NED**          And I didn't.
**ELIZABETH**    No.

*Pause.*

**NED**          I've never met... like you... anyone.
I don't want to be forgiven. I didn't come here to be
forgiven, and I don't think I deserve to be forgiven. But
I want to... help. *(Pause.)*
**ELIZABETH**    He was going to give it all up, he told me,
the night before, when I was there. *(She starts to see it
all. Her dad enters, and goes through the checking-in
process.)* He arrived, went through the door, checked
in, signed the registration card.
**WILLIAM**      Thank you. Oh and I'm expecting a visitor,
my daughter. If she comes to reception, would you
send her up? Good.

*He continues on the journey through the hotel to the
room.*

**ELIZABETH**    Foyer, lift, fifth floor, doors open, corridor,
room.
**WILLIAM**      Room 533.
**ELIZABETH** *(To Ned)* Your room.
**NED**          My room.
**ELIZABETH**    And hiding there already, your bomb.
**NED**          My bomb.

*Elizabeth's father unpacks and then settles down with some paper work. (Marnie is in the room, too)*

**ELIZABETH**     I arrived later, saw him, we made up, and your bomb was there, with us, waiting to go off. I was in the room with the bomb. He said, next time we meet he said... oh, lots of things. You'd gone.

**NED**     Twenty-four days previous. I was well away, watching the news on the telly.

**ELIZABETH**     And your bomb in there with him...

*Elizabeth's father kicks off his shoes, loosens his tie, sits at the desk and gets out a stack of paper. He starts to read and make some notes.*

*The buzzing grows louder and louder. Elizabeth looks at Ned, frightened.*

*In the hotel, Marnie stands alone.*

**MARNIE**     Mum, this room. I'm scared. Mum.

*She is on her own.*
*The buzzing grows and grows. Then stops. After three seconds the bomb goes off – an enormous noise.*

*William is thrown off the chair in the hotel room; Marnie is thrown to the floor; Elizabeth is thrown off the chair she is on in the neutral house. Ned sits there, the explosion going on inside him and around him. He sees the two women.*

*They are covered with debris and dust. The noise of sirens and panic. William has gone.*

**ELIZABETH** *(Yelling)* Daddy! *(She claws through the rubble.)* Daddy... *(She searches and searches and calls for help.)*

*She continues searching, scrabbling through it all, finds a briefcase, a shoe, a watch. She holds it to her ear. It is still ticking. She cannot find him. She is sprawled amongst utter chaos. Ned offers his hand to lift her up, but she gets up without him. Her hand is shaking.*

*She starts to walk. Marnie and Ned watch her.*

**ELIZABETH** *(Fast as it floods back)* That day, in the street after the bomb. I'm walking, I'm walking. I can't walk normally, I don't know how to walk, my hand, I can't stop it. I tell myself: 'My dad's dead. My dad's dead'. My world has died and a wall's come up.
Two builders yelling at me.
'Come on, love, it can't be that bad.'
But it is. My dad's dead. My dad's dead. My dad's dead.

**MARNIE**      Door. Corridor. Lift. Down, down, down. Foyer, through the door. I'm just going out for some air.

*Exit Marnie.*

*Elizabeth is back with Ned in the present.*

**ELIZABETH**     You don't go and meet the man who killed your father. It's not what you do.

**NED** *(Standing, in the midst of it all)* I'm trying to put into words. The feelings that are coming to me. I'm responsible for things and I have to live with that. Some day I may be able to forgive myself. Although I still stand by my actions. I have to grapple with the fact that I hurt human beings.

**ELIZABETH**     Marnie says to tell you you're a bad man, a bad man for killing Grandad.

*This hits him hard.*

**NED**     I have hidden behind a reduced view. Not seeing the individual.

*Pause. She looks into him.*

**ELIZABETH**     I'm glad it was you.

*They are drained.*

**NED**     You OK? *(Elizabeth nods.)*
**ELIZABETH**     What now?
**NED**     It's late. I'm cream crackered.
     *(He walks to the door, then turns.)*
     I'm really sorry I killed your father.

*He goes.*
*The sound of the sea and seagulls calling.*
*Music.*

**THE BOMB**

*Elizabeth bends down and finds in the rubble an old plastic cup and a lolly stick. She throws them away. Then she finds a bucket.*
*She finds her dad's briefcase and sand spills out of it. She fills the bucket and starts to build a sandcastle. She finds a scrap of paper, tears it into a flag and puts it in the top. She is crying – the first and only time we see her do so.*

*Marnie comes to her and holds her then stands in front of the sea. She kicks off her shoes. She walks towards the sea. Steps in. It is freezing.*

**MARNIE**        Fwoooorh! No way!

*But after the shock, she smiles, giggles. She swims. She is free.*

*Elizabeth watches her smiling.*
*The end.*